An Auto-Erotic
History of Swings

For Fred —

An Auto-Erotic
History of Swings

PATRICIA YOUNG

*with all best
wishes with
your writing*

sononis
PRESS

SONO NIS PRESS • WINLAW, BRITISH COLUMBIA

Patricia

LIBRARY AND ARCHIVES CANADA CATALOGUING IN PUBLICATION
Young, Patricia, 1954-
    An auto-erotic history of swings / Patricia Young.

Poems.
ISBN 978-1-55039-178-7

    I. Title.

PS8597.O673A78 2010   C811'.54   C2010-905255-2

Sono Nis Press most gratefully acknowledges support for our publishing
program provided by the Government of Canada through the Book
Publishing Industry Development Program (BPIDP) and the Canada
Council for the Arts, and by the Province of British Columbia through the
British Columbia Arts Council and the Book Publishing Tax Credit,
Ministry of Provincial Revenue.

Edited by Michael Kenyon
Copy edited by Merrie-Ellen Wilcox
Proofread by Karla Decker
Cover and interior design by Jim Brennan
Cover image: Ancient Art & Architecture Collection/GetStock.com

Published by
SONO NIS PRESS
Box 160
Winlaw, BC V0G 2J0
1-800-370-5228

books@sononis.com
www.sononis.com

Printed on acid-free paper that is forest
friendly (100% post-consumer recycled
paper) and has been processed chlorine free.

Printed and bound in Canada by
Houghton Boston Printing.

The Canada Council | Le Conseil des Arts
for the Arts | du Canada

For Terence

Table of Contents

The Art of Love

Karita in Love (again)

God's Last Words

The Art of Love

The Art of Love

*Cadmus Milesius . . . wrote fourteen great volumes on the passion of
love, but they are not now to be found.*

Where are they, those misplaced manuals?
Dropped in the Ganges?
Buried inside an Abyssinian crypt?
Inadvertently packed into orange crates,
sent to a Venetian market? Pushed to the back
of a stable in northern Scotland, where for eight hundred years
only the Clydesdale horses with their great round rumps
pawed at their existence? The Kama Sutra says
the art of love is the art of pleasing women,
and a nineteenth-century English surgeon said
the man who simply *fucks* is like the man who,
listening to a Beethoven sonata on the violin,
hears only a nag's tail scraping against a sheep's entrails.
But what, I'd like to know, did Cadmus Milesius say?
Imagine him in tunic and sandals, seated at a small wooden table,
holding a stylus between thumb and index finger,
recording for posterity a timeless sexual wisdom.
Should we devote our lives to searching
for his vanished texts or should we start again,
at the beginning, transcribing the courtship
of dragonflies, for instance, the male's exceeding
consideration toward the female whose thorax he longs
to grasp with his legs? Should we lie on the dock on a summer
afternoon, observing this bog skimmer's tender
preliminaries, his diffident, aerial approach?

Moments After My Conception

The importance of antenatal puericulture was fully recognized in China a thousand years ago.

My mother lay on a rattan mat, legs straight
as chopsticks. She did not march out of the city
carrying a sword and shield. She was too busy

reciting poems that brought tears to her eyes.
For nine months she spat hairpins inlaid
with kingfisher feathers at the demons

snarling at the outer gate. Wore jute sandals.
Pinched her nostrils when passing fresh ox dung
on the road. On market days she'd cross the bridge

back and forth, gold bells tied to her ankles. Or,
sitting upright in a bamboo chair, she'd consort
with celestial creatures. She was magnificent

as a sacrificial rooster, unblinking as the toad
at the bottom of the well. Mornings, she'd beat
a pigskin drum to chase away the rabid dogs.

Afternoons, she'd embroider images of kylin
on the back of my little jackets. She would not
gossip or wade into dreams rotting with fish heads.

If her rice was not sculpted into perfect squares
she would not eat. If her teacup did not glow like
the moon she would not drink. Her gaze swooped

like a swallowtail. Her toes spread like the roots
of the sui wood tree. From every branch and hook
she hung ladles painted with half-human, half-bird

grotesques. On the eighth day of the first lunar
month my mother, born in the remote mountains
of Sichuan province, turned her back on the evil

spirit disguised as a blind beggar. She filled
her mouth with pebbles and sang my talents
and virtues through the coldest night of winter.

Her auspicious thoughts conjured two white tigers.
Under her pillow: a knife engraved with *Longevity*.
A bunch of foxtail millet sprang from each breast.

What We Know About Babies

Most children . . . are in possession of a theory of the origin of babies.

They come from cow patties and God's solar-
powered kitchen, though we suspect the Holy Mother
drops them into doctors' bags along with wasps'
nests and rattlesnakes. Or the midwife will go
up in a balloon to fetch a little squalling thing
back to earth swaddled in a tea towel. You can

order a blue baby from the winter catalogue.
Last Christmas Santa came ho-ho-ho-ing down a ladder
and plunked them in all the empty mailboxes.
The colicky ones, well, they come from the ears
of sows. Some curl inside the sticky buns
you can buy in Chinatown. I know this because

last week I pulled apart the steaming dough and found one,
half-formed, sleeping in a gooey bed of jam.
Don't believe the rumour that babies come from
the torsos of many-breasted beasts. And those
human shapes growing inside the abandoned cars
in Hagar's Field? What else could they be?

They arrive suddenly, like hiccups, wearing nothing
but wool booties and brittle bats' wings that snap
in the first frost. They can tread water and hold
their breath longer than mermaids, though we doubt
angels drop the wizened ones in puddles to plump them up
like gooseberries. What happens to those loved briefly,

then discarded, do they end up as firewood? Once,
I heard a baby mew all night in a cardboard box.
And this I know is true: the milkman delivered one
to the crazy lady on Broom Lane when her husband
was at sea. We used to think the stork brought babies
but now only the gullible among us believe the frog

writhing in the bird's bill is a tiny human infant.
Our big-boned mother tells beautiful lies, but she
would never lie to us about the baby she dug out of
the ground along with the potatoes. See how firmly
she holds the squirmy thing under the basement tap
to wash away the worms and bugs and clumps of dirt.

Taboo-Girl

Intercourse during menstruation . . . has everywhere been
overlaid by the ideas of a culture which has insisted on regarding
menstruation as a supernatural phenomenon which, for the
protection of everybody, must be strictly tabooed.

Outside the door old women are beating the bushes
with sticks, angry, angry, they are beating
the reptile that made me bleed.
Do I look scared? Ha! I am Taboo,
last hurrah priestess, girl with an angelic roar.

Milk sours. Wine turns to vinegar. Sugar blackens. Meat rots.

Father says, *Now look what you've done.*
Mother says, *Get back in your cage.*

Come near me and sand fleas will sting your ankles.
And yet the sight of my breasts calms the sea.
Cowed by my nakedness, lightning
cracks, Holy Dove flies in my face.

Once I was half boy.
That was before Lizard-God cut us down the middle.
Now I'm married to Snake. Now I keep
yanking his tail out of my mouth.

When I walk into the world
vermin fall from the ears of corn,
caterpillars drop from curled leaves.

Father says, *Don't touch the ground, don't look at the sun.*
Mother says, *Cut your hair, burn your soiled clothes.*

What does it mean, this theatre of fire and blood?
Electricity sparking from my fingertips?

When no one's looking I get down on my haunches
and push – *uh-nuh uh-nuh uh-nuh.* Out slips
Salamander-Baby covered in slime.
I roll her down the road and into
the lime kiln. All night Baby bakes like clay.

Playing Ma and Pa

"Playing at pa and ma" is indeed extremely common among children in genuine innocence, and with a complete absence of viciousness; and is by no means confined to children of low social class.

Let them rake leaves behind the old cotton mill.
In ratty T-shirts let them shout
crude endearments
back and forth
in the bright chill air. Let Ma pause
to look up at the jet stream,
the distant river. Let blue autumn gold saturate Pa's skin.
Let the maple leaves change colour on the trees
as Ma rakes those already fallen.
Without adjectives, let Pa describe
each leaf as it spins to the ground
on a sun-charged wheel.
Let Ma heap the leaves into a higher and higher pile.
Let their rakes drag the earth.
Let them work side by side
in the field behind the old cotton mill
as people have always worked –
in rhythm, in silence, in the company of a friend.
Let the ghosts of their great-grandparents,
bent over spinning machines,
unbend
and step off windowsills
into the half-light of evening.

Let Ma gape.
Let Pa fall backwards
onto the bed they have raked into being.
Let them roll around on that bed,
Pa on top of Ma, Ma on top of Pa.
Behind an abandoned brick building
let them punch and squeal and pull each other's hair.

Portal

It very commonly happens, for instance, in all civilized countries
that the navel is regarded as the baby's point of exit from the body . . .

Hush, child, it's nothing
 but a rag-knot,
bump-gnarl, insect-lair,
 and no, you can't
lose it, catch it, bury it
 underneath the oak
tree, don't worry, it's harmless,
 hapless, a glub-nut, pin-
prick, glob-nob, dung-bun,
 squirt-drop, a whisper soft as . . .
shhhh, darling, just a pearl-
 stitch, thimble-crumb, tear-
ditch, rinky-dink, snicker-
 spur, best to ignore it, outwit
it, unknow it – what? –
 through *that* tiny portal, *that*
wee cave? Sweetheart! It's
 your own little jam pot,
kiss-wink, scar-tar, nubble-
 bubble, berry-squish, and, no,
it won't sting you, bite you, jump
 out and poke you, it's stuck
there, a burl-blot, turban-bud,
 bulge-mash, sleep, child,
it's just a tad-blip, flesh-lump,
 boogly-button.

Night-Running

*Trial-marriages ... [allow] the young couple to spend the night
together ... Night-courtship flourishes in stable and well-knit
European communities not liable to disorganization by contact with
strangers.*

Tarrying, the Irish called it, *handfasting, bundling.*
In Holland they *quested.* The Norwegians said *night-running,*
and no wonder, the great distances between them,
the boy loping

across his father's fields, plunging into the dank
pine forest, flowering lingonberry and tysbast, whisky
rags streaking the sky, running out to the western
edge, grass slapping his ankles, kittiwakes and whooper
swans, the blood in his head bright as the sun
that will not go down.
The girl hangs

out her bedroom window. Last Sunday
during hymns he turned and looked straight
at her, *O Jesus, Sweet and Lowly,* his look was a hot
summer wind that blew her wide open. He's still a land mile away
but she can feel the earth's tremor, his feet pounding
closer, his body

               springing
                     forward
and then a shadowy figure emerges from the trees,
slowing   breathing hard   circling the woodpile.
He kicks

a stone as though he just happened by,
and is that her moving behind the curtain?

A ladder leans against the house.
He climbs and enters, stands before her,
an awkward offering. *Now what,* his tongue-tied
hands seem to ask. If her heart's beating madly he does not
hear it, if she throws back the quilt he'll take off
his boots, but what else can he take
off, the rules are the rules.

                          Who are they,

this girl sitting upright against the pillows,
prim as a matron about to serve tea, this boy
whose hair smells of grilled dogfish?
Sweat runs down
his back and he tells her he's warm,
running so far, would she mind if he removed
his shirt. Well, she's warm too, this heavy skirt,
these scratchy leggings. They turn
from each other to un-
button,
turn
and turn back
newly born
skin rucked over bone,

but still they don't touch,

lie side by side on her straw mattress,
listening to the timbers settle and creak, silence
so huge it swells up to the rafters and breaks into
talk. They talk for hours,
                              talk
nonsense in her high narrow bed, talk
until dawn and her father's boots clomp past the door,
down the stairs, and then the crack

of the axe blade,
dry clatter of kindling, talk into
next week, next month, bonfires and feasting, schnapps
and maypoles. *So who will you dance with?*
she asks, her thigh
                    brushing his thigh,
      an accident
to which there's no answer, there's nothing more
to say now the world has become
thigh, now thigh

is the only word they know:
a night road lit up by candles, garden of sweet mosses,
dull thrum vibrating against the roof of their skulls.

The Great Peasant Girls

The child cannot remain asexual "when he sees the great peasant girls,
as ardent as mares in heat, abandoning themselves to the arms of
robust youths."

Where:

Aloft haystacks. Before open hearths.
Looking through slit windows.
On the dirt floors of the cruck houses
our fathers built out of wattle and daub.
In parish graveyards. Surrounded by wild swans.
At the tail end of weather-bitten dreams.
Inside a woodpecker's drum rap.
Astride skeletal winds. At the bottom
of the feudal system. Between the warm bodies
of cows. Beyond the village of our squabbling
imaginations. Against honeycomb walls.
On our grannies' deathbeds.
Beneath the mourner's gloom.
Approaching a rock stile, having paused mid-step
to scratch an ankle. Inside dried-up river basins.
In noblemen's orchards, our heads lost among the fallen apples.

Who:

The clodhopper in wooden clogs.
The boy who sharpened the knives and other murderous tools.
The blacksmith's sons, their lips branding us with kisses.
The tall one in goatskin cape and woollen socks.
The innkeeper's boy, who, having publicly
cursed the tax, was fined the tax six times over.
The earl himself. The miller's bandy-legged nephew
with his quiver of arrows. The idiot boy
whittled down to a raft of bones. The one caught

barefoot, acorns in his pocket, rabbit in his sack.
The baker's sons rising around us like sweet dough.
The priest who passed over our souls
but likened our breasts to the vowels of angels.
The weaver's brother, his near-drowning
a baptism that failed to disturb the loom's rocking.
The one who arrived in a snowstorm like a gift from God.

Why:

Because our lives were tallow candles.
Because a chunk of stale bread and raw onion.
Because inhaling and exhaling had become a habit.
Because a boy's nimble fingers. Because the sound
of ice melting in spring was the sound
of our mothers' keening: another mouth to feed,
another baby dead. Because we were loose,
immoral, unholy. Because threshing and winnowing
in our masters' fields. Because we loved air
more than water and water more than meat.
Because the laws written with our blood
were the laws we kept breaking. Because hooks
unhooked themselves and light drained from the sky.
Because we tarried a brief moment in the devil's
house and when we came out we said
it was much like we imagined heaven.

First Kiss

Even by ballet dancers and actresses on the stage, [drawers] were not invariably worn.

My pretty French friend, so theatrical, declaims,
Drawers! Moi! A respectable girl from Paris?
then pulls on Oriental
unmentionables.

Are we men?
Immodest, unfeminine?
Flesh-coloured *caleçons* beneath our muslin skirts?
Drawers that descend below the knee?

(In 1807 the farthingale dropped
from women's bodies
and prostitutes'
undergarments
were not of this world;
their other-worldly cotton
drawers reached Europe through Crete,
that weirdly embroidered
channel of communication.)

Tonight, we're thirteen and in love
with shapely novelties
dare to touch tongues, slug
to slug, strange, unearthly sensation,
like coming to life on a salt flat
or riding bareback across a volcanic plain.

Three Poems About Scent

1. The Problem of Describing Scent

Even among savages the perfuming of the body is sometimes
practiced with the object of inducing love in the partner.

If I said seven girls gathering leaves from seven gum trees.
If a bundle of dried sage hung around the old chief's neck.
If the summer season in the sleeping house.

If three boys returning from the forest
with aromatic creepers, gifts
for their sweethearts.

If a mother lying beside her baby, singing –
My little sachet of moss.
My little sachet of ferns.

If floors strewn with sweet grasses.

If I said burn the aloe wood for its aromatic smoke.
If I listed twenty-seven plants including ylang-ylang.

If a young woman alone in a room,
rosewater sprinkled in her hair,
jasmine flowers scattered on her bed.

If the beloved waiting
patiently (patiently)
outside her door.

2. Young Love

. . . in many persons – usually, if not exclusively, women – the odor of flowers produces not only a highly pleasurable, but a distinctly and specifically sexual, effect . . .

These days when I step into the street,
working my way through the city's traffic,
there's sometimes a whiff of bergamot or
sassafras, a hint of camphor. Smells like
the smells I smelled when our love was
new and incorruptible, and I wonder, is it
that time of year again, the world gushing
green life? The dull male moth releasing
its mango scent, ants dancing on the heads
of peony buds, coaxing their fragrance into
bloom. Sometimes lately the air's redolent
with the sandalwood soap I lathered on your
back, or a perfume I wore when summer after-
noons smelled of mown hay. Or, walking out
after rain, I startle – a trace of your scent – and
my mouth opens again to those wild and weeping
nights we suffered the heartless white flowers.

3. A City Called Musk

Thus, the old English physician . . . remarked that "several delicate
women who could easily bear the stronger smell of tobacco have been
thrown into fits by musk . . . "

Let's say we travelled a long distance,
from indolence and black skies,
asylums and great houses, ailing,

dragging our feet, that we arrived
heavy with torpor in this city of
winding, narrow streets with names

like Musk-Ox and Musk-Mole,
that each back alley was imbued with
its own shadows and eclipses, the dark

cafés lit up by small cups of muscatel.
Let's say only plants that gave off
the noblest fragrances – musk-rose,

musk-hyacinth, musk-orchid –
flourished on the rooftop terraces.
That donkeys laden with baskets

of dates and nuts trotted past the souks.
Leather slippers, throw pillows, Berber
rugs, candelabras, bolts of blue silk.

All the delights of the Islamic world
simmering inside magic boxes.
Let's say we ambled through botanical

gardens, the branches overhanging
the tiled walkways weighted with figs;
a belly dancer in a fez, strumming

a three-string guitar. Even the jugglers
and storytellers radiated a natural perfume –
musk-cherry, musk-rat, musk-duck.

Let's say our hearts contracted when
a camel knelt before us, emitting a musky
odour from its facial glands, that our

groin muscles spasmed when the healer's
voice addressed each one of us
as *my dear Henrietta*. Let's say

a powerful dose of deer musk jolted
our nervous system. Say shudder,
say paroxysm, say heliotropic swoon.

Luminous

A girl may be a perfect model of outward decorum and yet have a very filthy mind. The prudishness with which she is brought up leaves her no alternative but to view her passions from the nasty side of human nature.

From the kitchen window, she watches
Henry Wittaker, respectable
neighbour's son, piss
like a dog against a fence post, and she's
had it with the fettered life, sweet-
faced and buttoned up. She wants hickeys
on her neck, floodlights and hallucinations,
everything luminous, drenched in revelatory
detail – coral slip-ons and a papier mâché
pig mask. The fire hydrant bursts. She flicks
her skinny braids, looks at the world
through pigeonhole eyes. *Henry,*
she sings. A trashy a cappella.

Initiation

*Among the Yuman Indians of California, as described
by Horatio Rust ... the girls are at puberty prepared for
marriage by a ceremony.*

Time to lie down in pits dug out of the earth,
strange death-time at the end of childhood, dry
tobacco leaves tickling our faces. Three days
and three nights, peering through wool blankets,
the old ones dancing around us, their wattled
arms and veined thighs. How our skin itches,
how we gaze at the stars. Time to listen to
gourd songs and songs of coyotes. Formless,
entombed in the ground, swaddled in warm
stones. Time of gifts and straw mats, the women
scattering piton nuts, moonlight illuminating
the upthrust stones. Giggling-time, the little girls
stomping around us, shaking deer-hoof rattles.
We wriggle like earthworms, grow bored as squash.
Dream-time in open graves, river-dreams and dreams
of tortoise lovers. Deep pause below the horizon,
and then blood-rush, time to rise up, shake off corpse-
dirt. Time to return to our bodies, think of boys as men.

Devil Lover

Isabel Gowdie, a Scotch witch, bore clear testimony . . . "The youngest and lustiest women," she stated, "will have very great pleasure in their carnal copulation with him, yea . . . He is abler for us than any man can be."

This morning I kicked away the snow to study the casual arrangement of stones. Your breath smouldered among the ashes, your hoof prints, frozen in mud. You are the one I cry out to in the night, the one I wear like a libidinous skin. When I was a girl my father tied my wrists to the bedposts, locked the doors to keep the boys out. Now you hex my husband's organ, make it disappear, then reappear in a gannet's nest. Sudden gusts hit the window. How much longer? At last, I hear you moving up the flue, your tail brushes my thighs, black wings enfold me, press me tighter, salivate on my breasts, probe the darkness between my legs, ravish me with your kisses, stab me, devour me, cut out my tongue, these yelps of joy.

The Sexual Significance of Birds

*These experiences may be regarded as fairly typical of the erotic dreams
of healthy and chaste young men. The bird, for instance, that changes
into a woman while retaining some elements of the bird . . .*

You burn for her
the way your tonsils once burned
after a swig of your daddy's home-brewed
whisky but when you reach out
to touch her
she scurries across the floor.

Her red feet and plump chest
more alluring
than the smell of fermenting mash.
You, a predator?
You, who long to roll in her grasses?
You chase after your game bird, grabbing at tail

feathers, but she lifts off the ground,
up up up to the rafters
where she perches
in the heavenly vapours. Strange
popping sounds, derisive laughter, your partridge
love drowning in a vat of bubbling corn mash.

And then you're walking down the street
beside a beautiful woman
in a purple hat and black stockings.
Her arms are elaborately tattooed. *It's me,*
she says, *Elijah Pepper's daughter from Jerusalem Ridge,*
and you confess you've never known

a woman, not really, not in the Biblical sense,
and she bobs her head, charmingly:
Kuta-kut-kut, kuta-kut-kut. A long glide and she bursts
into a whir of beating wings. Oh god,
you can't help yourself,
plunge both hands in.

The Female Flirt

... there is another form in which the art of love is largely
experimented and practised, especially in England and America,
the form of flirtation.

Early psychiatrists denounced the flirt as a degenerate
but I like the provocative glances at gas station
pumps, the vertical scan in library mezzanines, flirts
parading back and forth among the stacks of world history:
Mata Hari and Cleopatra, infamous flirts sashaying
through the centuries, tossing out non-verbal cues.

Flirts flirt; it's what they do best. They're hip-tilters,
body-anglers, say, *I'd love to stay but have to go.*
My mail carrier's a flirt. So are the inner-city
cops strutting the beat in bulletproof vests.
In a state of full flirtage they assume scandalous
positions and endure loss with more grace
than your average risk-taker. Only the flirt
has the courage to stride through a barroom
brawl, batting her lashes. What archeologist
doesn't long to unearth the lost civilization of flirts?

They have names like Darlene and Belinda
but don't misunderstand them, they don't want
to run off to Waikiki with you. They're just curious,
alive to nuance. Look, there's one now, sidling
up to the man bent over a secondhand-book
bin. When he swivels in her direction,
she pops up like a jam tart. Suddenly
everything's slightly hilarious.

In hospital corridors the flirt radiates
a deeply alluring glow. Though death gurneys
around her she pouts and primps, arches her back.
Incorrigible in subway stations, running up
the down escalator. Her come-hither look
says what others can only stammer into words.

Flirts are indifferent to caveats and the pitfalls of courtship,
never cocky or superficial. Their annihilating winks
and high-voltage smiles zap the unsuspecting heart.
Give out their phone numbers? Refuse
a martini? *Not so fast,* they say with their eyes.
I don't want you, Loverboy, I just want you to want me.

Ruthless, incandescent, more beautiful than ordinary women.
Watch them hike up their skirts and beat back the abyss.
Four million years ago the first flirt walked upright
onto the savannah, palms open, throat exposed.

Feral

... the sexual climaxes of spring and autumn are rooted in animal procreative cycles ...

The great white horses stamp
their ancestral hooves until the wind sings
black clover and the thunderous bulls
rampage the moon-bright pastures and *come*
to me with your face full of heartbreak
purr the spotted leopards in the wine-deep
caves and the operatic goats take the formless
world into their mouths while the land bleats
the vernal equinox and women's uteruses
contract at lunar intervals recalling
a time when the sun's virgin daughters
dreamed tumescent dreams and the ferret
bitch slides into the marsh while the rutting
stags emerge from steaming rivers into bodies
more feral than the pot-bellied pigs running
amok and the wolves howl a cosmic reckoning
backdrop to the elephants trumpeting a saturnalia
in the waning spring light while the hyenas
lick their mates' paws in the increasingly
debauched season and the promiscuous
chimpanzees use their human hands to shake
their tambourines at the llamas rising from
the earth's sandy bed and the moon ejaculates
white nectar startling the scarlet tanagers
their tiny orange skirts twirling in the branches.

They Touch for the First Time

*The lower we descend in the animal scale, the more varied we find
the functions of the skin . . .*

In the old feather-and-tongue game she gave blood-jump,
nerves, viscera, sense-muscles, ping! Smoother than,
softer, more pliable, durable under exposure. So
steel, he gave, tough and elastic. Ancient,
she gave, caresses, tender, resistant:
electric currents. Cell by cell, he descending,
down to infant-time, womb-dwelling,
simple complexities grazed the possible.
She gave fundamental, mother of all senses,
slid further, fingertips, latent energy,
primary conditions. Suddenly he gave
and this skin thing happened: humidity
and drought, cold and heat, neck hairs, ear
of heaven. Danger-proof, she gave, embryonic
enfoldings. Surface hum, he gave, inadequate qualifier.
How say alabaster, ivory, cream, silk, velvet?
All inferior. Delirious, she gave, light shedding,
sensory impression, reflex, lips first. Organic, he gave,
spinal cord, brain-channel, that shape. Response
and wonder: what they were wrapped in: fine-weave,
body sheath, more impervious than rubber.

In the 3-D Garden

The inexperienced bride cannot know beforehand that the
frequently repeated orgasms which render her vigorous and radiant
exert a depressing effect on her husband, and his masculine pride
induces him to attempt to conceal that fact.

The bride in her innocence rises
early to the challenge of pornographic
art, rises to the knothole above her head,
breasts and hips rising with each inhalation,
a line of pure pleasure. The bride is
an ordinary fruit-dove carved out of stone,
loves the orange-bellied wompoo, loves
the sphinx moth's pink hind wings.
Before a full-length mirror assesses
her head circled in lancelike florets,
judges herself abstractly, a kind of soft core
version of *innocent bride,* comic book
character who answers to the name
of *Blushing Peach Stalk.* Not even her husband
can fragment her ardour; not even he
can tamp down the too-passionate
bride rising at the mouth
of the garden like a stately blue
lupine committed
to another conceptually loaded sin.

A Question of Frequency

The general ignorance concerning the art of love may be gauged by the fact that perhaps the question in this matter most frequently asked is the crude question [of] how often sexual intercourse should take place.

A Hindu physician prescribed intercourse six times a week
except during the torpid season
when the coral snails creep out of their holes
and the tiger butterfly is more prevalent than catfish.
The Talmud imposed intercourse upon the healthy
but idle man once every thirty-two hours.
Russian priests argued against excess
for with excess comes delusions and baldness.
A ninth-century monk stumbled out of the forest,
singing like a dark-eyed junco, then decreed
intercourse thirteen days out of every month.
The Archbishop of Canterbury slept on and on.
Years later he woke to announce he'd travelled to the city
where Charlemagne's knight boasted one hundred times
in twenty-four hours with Constantinople's daughter
(her laughter turned mythic and took her father's breath away).
Swiss doctors advised the man in his prime
to stand beneath a rainspout in a downpour
before a breakfast of sausage and strong stout.
At least six times a day, declared the Florentine Ambassador
for he had been raised on gravity and other fantastic hypotheses.
A country preacher boomed from his Tennessee pulpit:
Do it X many times according to the moss growing
on your stonewalls and if moss does not grow
on your stonewalls do it according to the hour
on your sundials and if there are no sundials
do it according to the women of the Great Smoky Mountains
who insist their menfolk put away their columns and calculations
that they might inhale the men's skin as they inhale the juniper's wood.

Conversation

... the foot bandage [is] strictly analogous to the waist bandage or corset which also tends to produce deformity of the constricted region.

Nobleman to His Favourite Concubine:

You astound me with your shy demeanour,
unfurl a discourse on the temple dogs
of Taou and Fo. Your mincing
steps entrance me while I
sleep you cast
a bitter aphrodisiac
on my forehead so that waking I
have eyes for only you
can prevail against my idleness,
acquaint me with the distant stars.
While others venerate grain and hemp
before the rural altars
you extol me
with your bells and banners.
Your naked foot more lovely
than a dwarf
tree stuns me like the human
face divine. Now you bow
before the rude emblems of the season,
assail me with your lotus garlands,
fold me in these plumes
of smoke, make
of your little feet a swallow's
nest I fly into.

Concubine's Response:

When I was small I didn't know I was small
and then my mother died. I broke my own
arch, forced heel and toe together (who,
if not me?). And now you come to my bed
with talk of forty-eight ways to play with
these three-inch lotuses. A white-tailed deer
steps out of the trees, then vaults back into
the forest. Pain? Honestly, I cannot remember it.

Short Takes on the Foot

Of all forms of erotic symbolism the most frequent is that which idealizes the foot and the shoe.

No smut, please.
The girls of Albania in long woollen stockings
are listening at the door.

*

As he bent to kiss
her pollen-dusted chopine,
he felt an orgasmic
sneeze
coming on.

*

Scandalous
the seated virgin, one knee placed over the other,
sacred foot exposed.

*

When a wealthy manufacturer
gifted a pair of embroidered shoes
with rhinestone buckles
to the king's bride,
the offer was rejected:
The queen of Spain has no legs!

*

Gold slipper, gilt bands, bodiless Etruscan foot.

*

By nightfall nothing was left but the elusive connection
between the Egyptian foot and sexual pleasure
as it once existed in the shadow of a pyramid.

*

Consider the sepia photograph
of a woman naked but for
silk mules. Consider
the woman,
her nakedness,
those mules.

*

Immodest medieval poulaines terminating in a bird's beak
followed by metal appendages
led to
the impudent invention of shoes in the shape of –
you guessed it.

*

That's some sexy sandal,
the ancient Greek senator said to the goddess
on his way to democracy.

*

Cinderella's glass slippers?
A metaphor for moth eggs?
Short feet on the take.

*

My great-great grandmother,
a Viennese prostitute, removed her ankle-laced boots
in the presence of a man with whom she was deeply in love.
Good god, he gasped. *What have you done?*

Riddle

"An erection," it has been said, "is a blushing of the penis."

I am not a sun-eater, though some of my best friends eat the sun.
If I had legs, I would walk to the aquarium.
Duct tape can't hold me together.
Upon reaching maturity, I've run out of fresh cells.
The boundary between you and me is less porous than you think.
My nicknames are Crackerjack and Beanpole.
In another life I was a green-skinned autotroph.
Think: submarine, teardrop.
I'm an unbridled coma, the antidote to apathy.
Check me out through blue blocker glasses.
I'm less important than photosynthesis
but more important than your field notes.
I evolved on Mars,
which might explain my interest in deep-sea diving.
I'm not an insect repellent or ultraviolet sunscreen.
I would like to sign your autograph.
In old age, I still act like a kid.
No one could accuse me of pushing up daisies.
During lapses in the conversation I find myself burrowing.
My love life is complicated by a certain rootedness.
I would like to meet fresh faces.
One minute I'm all whimsy, the next all whim-wham.
I'm only one half of a riotous equation.
The barely decipherable figure of a woman picking flowers
in a botanically explicit field piques my interest.
I live in a perpetual state of expectation.
A mole has better eyesight.
I would never shoot myself, even in self-defence.
The tug of evaporation – water droplets pulled up from the soil
through hollow capillaries moves me
to tears. O to shinny
ever skyward!

The Littlest Orgasm

*A Brahmin woman informed a medical correspondent in India that she
had distinct though feeble orgasm . . . if she stayed long near a man whose
face she liked, and this is not uncommon among European women.*

The littlest orgasm rocks the dawn.
It goes rat-a-tat-tat.
It mails itself to a country where the butter
is yellow and the bees return
to pollinate the clover.
It floats possibilities.
During fluke snowstorms it weeps latex tears.
It is not aerodynamic after all.
It descends the Eiffel Tower, disappointed as anyone.
It stands too close to the catwalk.
And coughs.
Orgasms come in all sizes but this one's the littlest.
The auctioneer can't sell it on the block.
The computer guy can't download it.
It lacks the bump, pizzazz, fireworks on the front lawn.
It meanders like a bedtime story.
It's a sweet thing to repeat and report, no small wonder.
It refuses to tongue-kiss on the red carpet.
It has skinny-dipping on its mind.
It's a high-wire act, a live-wire hum.
It looks in all the obvious places.
It's, like, I be marching for freedom, yo.
It will not be ignored, uh-uh, its heart is made up.
Where's its pin-up boy, where its shoe-shine girl?
Not a birdwatcher but it *is* ridiculously hip.
How perfectly it lines up the bow with the arrow.

It objects to life inside a matchbox.
It harbours grandiose dreams.
It noodles down country roads.
It shoots the air full of dirt pellets.
It praises the genuinely praiseworthy.
It writes in its diary: *cave spelunking, cave spelunking, cave spelunking.*
It's alive and well in Mazunte.
I'm gonna bust out of here, it says, just watch.

Masturbation: Q & A

[Masturbation] is found among the people of nearly every race of which
we have any intimate knowledge, however natural the conditions under
which men and women may live.

What is it, exactly?
A plagiarist's tale. Think: Heathcliff as Master of the Universe.

Is it a degenerative disease?
More like showbiz and a little black dress.

Does it lead to an aversion to sex?
Let us consider science and literature and the possibility of orbiting the
earth.

What percentage of the population engages in it?
Annie Clouster possesses nine recipes for bread and butter pudding.

What is meant by onanism?
You might as well accuse a boy of scratching his ear when it itches.

Is it more common among the fertile or the insane?
Would you mind if I put my tongue in there? he asked politely.

Can an addiction be broken?
The majority of beekeepers haven't the slightest interest
in raising a finger.

Does it feed into pornographic fantasies?
Ninety-nine per cent of the population has already confessed.
The other one per cent are liars.

Is it a slow form of suicide?
In the hottest part of the day, Annie Clouster gives herself up
to the throw-away lover.

Does it cause health problems?
Kiss me, do.

What did the pastor who condemned it as a sin hope to achieve?
Intimations of rock and roll.

Is it a substitute for sex?
Ask the unionized city workers
who report making hay while the sun shines.

Does infantile thumb-sucking lead to it?
Long ago a race of antique dealers passed into blissful degeneracy.

What evolutionary purpose to it?
On the day God and his Wife
were creating man and woman,
He asked to see his consort's handiwork.
She refused and slapped his hand.

During pregnancy ought one to refrain?
Floral arrangements, Annie Clouster scoffed.
A few sprigs! The odd fern!

Do women indulge in it with more imaginative fervour than men?
Consider the great Russian novelist
who wrote a dreamy sort of melancholy prose.

How assess a creature capable of making love to itself?
High art. High art, indeed.

The Cult of the Bath

It required very little insight and sagacity for the Christians to see...
that the cult of the bath was in very truth the cult of the flesh.

My love is Tahitian, clean, clean.
Three times a day he swims in the lagoon.
I rinse the salt from his limbs and when he opens his eyes
a tuna fish is flying across the sky.

He swims in the lagoon three times a day.
No masseuse or slave with strong hands
rides a tuna fish across the sky.
Or my love scrapes his skin with a metal tool. In the steam room

where he melts beneath his slave's strong hands.
Only a Roman could exult so fulsomely in his own beauty.
In the steam room he scrapes his skin with a curved metal tool.
Or my love is a lice-infested Christian,

no beautiful pagan: fulsome, exultant.
He clanks across the medieval wasteland in a dirty coat of mail,
this lice-infested Christian who loves
to preach a pure soul cannot inhabit a pure body.

He clanks across the medieval wasteland in a dirty coat of mail,
my holy man who cultivates filth for the sake of heaven.
Only an impure body can house a pure soul. Who
can save him – damned to hell for washing his own feet?

My holy man, who cultivates filth for the sake of heaven,
refuses to rinse the salt from his limbs, and when I open my eyes –
his god has damned him to hell for washing his own feet.
My Tahitian lover, however, is clean, clean.

The Tulip Tree

Religious prostitutes... [were] connected with temples in southern India...

Tears sprang into my mother's eyes
when the priest consecrated our union.
That I, waif in ankle bracelets,
had been chosen among so many.
I danced around his buttressed trunk,
crushed his leaves against my breasts.
The villagers cried out as though a great
joy had entered their bodies like rain.

For seven years I have been married
to the tree, yes, the tulip tree that stands
in the temple courtyard – furrowed bark
and narrow crown, horn-shaped buds
bejewelling his highest branches.

Tonight devotees traipse to my door,
their terrible thirst sloshing back and forth
in goatskin flasks. How can I refuse
these pilgrims who worship at the shrine
and receive the gods' blessings? *They*
are my sacred calling. And yet I pray
for the day when the tree is my only lover.
When I can lie beneath him in the afternoon
heat, his foliage and droopy scarlet
bells, ah, my throat streaked with pollen.

Dildo

The use of an artificial penis in solitary sexual gratification may be traced down from classic times, and doubtless prevailed in the very earliest human civilization . . .

Praise to the girls of Sumatra who praised you after
the boys took to their boats to pull fish out of the sea.

In the ashes of Pompeii you were buried along with
three ruby-studded combs, and so praise to archaeological

treasures and the green and pleasant lands in which
women fondled you openly in the marketplace. Praise

to the new moon and the widow's eldest daughter
who washed you with her tears. In Neolithic times

you were fashioned out of stone, then praised in private
conversation as an *exquisite delight.* Nothing new under

the sun, the Creole women of Venezuela sighed before
falling back to earth. So here's to the Parisian prostitutes

who praised you trippingly in their velvet boudoirs.
Praising your rosin suppleness, an eighteenth-century

abbess sold you for a leg of mutton. After her death
the letters kept coming: *Send quickly, the moments are*

pressing and I have been waiting too long. In China,
wealthy courtesans dropped their paintbrushes to offer

your praises through another watery afternoon. *Engi,*
the fashionable geishas said: instrument of pleasure and

grace. Elizabethan women filled you with praise and
warm milk before climbing into their husbands' cold beds.

Though no one, not even Freud, praised you for calming
the hysterics, women with dilated eyes fixed on the stars.

Sculpted in ancient Babylon, you now reside in a London
museum in a secret cabinet where none but a hipster

custodian can offer her praise. The aristocratic women of
northern Europe declared their love for you greater than

their love of food or wine or the horses on which they
rode bareback across the wind-bitten steppes. A ravishing

Dutch girl, the story goes, woke from a coma, blinked
twice, then shrieked your praises. In classical times you

sprang up on door knockers and lamps, evoking praise
and laughter, and sometimes you appeared as ebony,

sometimes ivory, sometimes wrapped in the folds of a tired
woman's skirts. The girls of Sri Lanka played Parcheesi

with tiny replicas of you while their mothers dabbled in
desultory games of chess. This too was a kind of praise.

And why not? said the Hawaiian women, impregnated
by elongated, curved fruits. Praise to all the impersonators,

the zucchinis and cucumbers, the horns strapped between
the legs of old women in Celtic mythology. How else to

interpret the dreams in which strange metamorphoses occur:
first you are pineapple, then amphibian, then African boar.

Praise to your rose-coloured beauty inside the Mongolian
woman's yurt, to the pole and crown, your wild-bird innocence.

Brass Eggs

Japanese women have probably carried the mechanical arts of auto-
erotism to the highest degree of perfection.

They say the lovesick women of the northern islands
would introduce two hollow balls the size of pigeons' eggs
into their vaginas. One empty. Inside the other
a heavy metal ball or a little quicksilver.

Tonight, lovesick yourself, you think
of those women rocking in rocking chairs, brass leaf balls
vibrating inside their bodies while outside beans climb trellises,
rain falls on rooftops, worlds tumble on.

Fruiting Bodies

The breath of Christian asceticism had passed over love; it was no longer, as in classic days, an art to be cultivated, but only a malady to be cured.

Dear Lord, let me not love the pungent mornings
she tromps through wet salal, hunting honeycomb

morels at the base of tree trunks, and if she arrives
on my doorstep with a kilo of puffballs, let me not

love her pail of fruiting bodies, or fall on my knees
for the hens of the woods that only moments earlier

knuckled through a composting stump. Rather,
let me hover on the smoky brink of my life, gazing

at heaven, and think not of the slippery jacks or
toothy-gilled hedgehogs she empties into my lap.

If during a late summer thunderstorm she roams
the dewy meadow, lifting this or that blanket to

uncover the cauliflower fungi, I will not look
upon her face, or crouch in the shaggy moonlight

where she gathers pine buttons. Nor will I drink the
stream water, nor breathe the musky air that carried

her like a lone spore to this island. O Lord, let me
unlove the wavy-capped one whom I love with a

fecund and overlapping joy. For even a glimpse
of her, muddy-kneed and bearing a sack of peppery

chanterelles, I would crawl through humus and dung
the length of three score and ten worlds. Pity me,

for I am sick as an old conk, darker than a truffle
buried in damp earth. For love of the mushroom

picker I lie on the forest floor and break down break
down break down into a pestilence of sweet rot.

Eve in Middle Age

Thus . . . it is the custom in Cornwall for country maids to eat the testicles of the young male lambs when they are castrated in the spring, the survival, probably, of a very ancient religious cult.

She's reading at the kitchen table when *testicle* appears before her eyes, not just testicle but testicle of male lamb castrated in spring and consumed as aphrodisiac. *Aphrodisiac?* A fruity word, surely, strawberry elixir, tiny black seeds, succulent cache. Not cruel, not bloody, not an animal's severed organs, though this could be naive on her part. She is a shamefully naive person. Believes Adam will come home, make love to her again. Rain pounds the tin roof. Tail end of a hurricane. A bowl of kiwis ripens on the counter. She reaches for a steak knife, splits a fuzzy brown egg down the middle. Cups a shell in her hand. And then the sound of gravel on the road, footsteps on the porch, key turning the lock. With two fingers she scoops out emerald green flesh, and *Come,* she says to the man dripping wet in the doorway. *Eat.*

Fisherwoman

*Sturdy peasant women . . . are inured to [cold water] . . . even
prolonged immersion . . . has no evil result . . . Their periods are
notably regular, and their fertility is high.*

My mother's walking the streets again in wet clothes,
hawking shrimp from her basket while
my brothers comb the beach, wrists wrapped in kelp.
Down by the boats, I ask, *Where is the boy
whose ear is a bottomless well?* I drop
a stone, wait for the splash. What I mean:
a face can be a dark blue sting.
Day after day my mother pushes against
the currents: O give us some peace,
our daily bread. It's the height
of summer; light streams down the dock.
We sit at the table and eat the same meal –
potatoes and fish, fish and potato.
Our plates quiver like jellied ponds.
Forgive me, I say to my brothers from my own narrow bed,
you're still young and already I'm lonely.
Their eyelids won't close so I tape them shut.
Before I know it I'm seventeen. So
this is what it feels like to be a mouse who wants to eat the moon.

An Auto-Erotic History of Swings

*... during the months when the men in these districts have to be
away from home the girls put up swings ...*

It was a custom of the Gilbert Islands
for a boy to push a girl on a rope-swing,
then leap up and enfold her in his arms and legs.

Ancient Samoans believed swinging ceremonies
promoted hallucinations as well as fertility
in the animal and vegetable kingdoms.

Young couples in the Philippines swung in late
afternoon, whereas the girls of New Guinea
pumped hardest in the hour before dawn.

After swinging, the Crow women of Montana
dreamed voluptuous encounters with the moon
in the shape of a man. Garden-variety swings

with flexible leather seats burned through
the pleated garments of Grecian women who
rode the succulent air – pelvises flexed, jaws

clenched, lips compressed. Swinging deep
in the rainforest, Yanomamö women warbled
bird calls to the men sleeping off their yopo

in grass-covered huts. A common sight in the
village squares of Germany: a little wooden
plank. On either side, rope hanging from a tree

branch. Yorkshire milkmaids were so chaste
they dared not voice their fantasies except when
alone, swinging from a barn's rafters. During

a three-day festival the women of the Songhees
tribe took turns pushing each other to greater heights.
Even a slight swaying can induce a transformative

experience, said the swampy women of the Mississippi
Delta. Swinging was popular among the peasant
girls of Sweden during the endless light. And

the magnificent women of Naples? Suspended
between heaven and earth, they'd throw back
their heads: *O sting of the flesh, O sweet consolation.*

Sacred

Thus an old Maori [asked], Who nowadays thinks of the sacredness of the head? See when the kettle boils, the young man jumps up, whips the cap off his head, and uses it for a kettle-holder.

The old Maori leaned against the wall of a barbershop on a side street lined with eucalyptus trees. *What will become of us?* he said. *The sacredness of the head, the hands, the feet, the buttocks.* Afternoon rain. Great white birds wheeling off the coast. He'd come for a wet shave, because the barber was good with a hot cloth and strop razor. Never a nick or burn. The boy in the barber's chair glanced up from his comic book. He looked in the mirror and did not smile. The men on the opposite bench smoked and told jokes and paid no attention to the old Maori, and the sound of snipping scissors sounded nothing like a weeping albatross. The barber swept the cape from the boy's body, then shook his own apron, quick storm of human hair, and no one but the old Maori understood that another sacred act had occurred at that time, in that place, only he remembered the lamps burning low, the women plunging naked, three times into the spring pool in the eucalyptus grove, the men anointing the women with kisses on their heads, hands, feet, buttocks.

Karita in Love (Again)

Fifteen

Met him at the Kissing Booth: three for a buck.
Wore my Girl Scout badges, who cares,
won the hula-hoop prize.

Cracked beer caps with my teeth,
torched the sumac bush outside the gym door.
Lay side by side on a basement floor.
Heard children's voices.
Sailed out to sea on the back of a dolphin.

Made apple soup for him, played gin rummy
on a dirty beige couch. Too young
for sex, but did that anyway.
Had seriously nutty thoughts.
Squirrelled them so far away
even I'd never find them.

Crawled blind across a parking lot.
He found my glasses, *he* laced up my Jesus sandals.
Saw God with him, saw God *in* him.
Strutted when I walked, howled when I wept.
Drank piss-coloured beer in a roadside bar.
If I was underage, too bad.

Was he your angel-star, your fin-de-siècle *lust?*
Don't talk to me about lust.
Was he your love-kick, your groove-note?
Don't talk to me about groove.

Retched into the wind.
Braids unravelled.
Stomach bulged like the moon.

Boys

Day-Glo idiots, hapless visionaries.
Boys were boys, we weren't particular.
Words bunched in their fists,
but what did we care? We wanted
the lazy and fuzzy-cheeked, the ones
who went ape-shit over girls who blew

smoke in their faces and came with six-month
warranties. Boys who made careers
out of playing the freak.
Winsome, awkward, brilliant. Why not?
Zen-boys with buttery apricot skin,
legs slung over our legs, purring like huge cats.

The fast talkers in sepia tones, the algebra
boys untangling the tangoed equation
at the heart of Latina girls. Our logic
was circular. We wanted them because
we wanted them. Let me explain
exactly what we had in mind: the quixotic

hardcore guitar pluckers, the sci-fi nerds
beaming radioactive light into our rec rooms.
Who wanted them? We did, us, the hippy chicks
and ice queens, the brainiacs and girls
so ordinary there was nothing to distinguish
us except the depth of our wanting.

The mind balks at how much,
how far back, and still we wanted to go
where they went, to not be afraid
of what they wanted. Boys loaded as

questions, simple as widgets. The sensitive
Lotharios in blazing white gym gear, the ones

who kept shooting themselves in the foot,
the mouth, into orbit. We tried to want
other things, fashion magazines, tennis lessons,
class C drugs, but nothing came close
to a sweetly vagrant boy inside a Goodwill
drop-off box. Whose fault was it?

That our kneecaps wanted them,
our mandibles, cartilage, tendons, ligaments,
you name it, every bit of us wanted them,
despite their roving eyes, their fumbling
monkey love. The more we wanted
boys, the more we wanted boys.

How dumb was that? To want the gritty
sex scene in them, the tryst, the future affair.
Boys who wanted us as much as we wanted them.
Or did they? We didn't ask. Didn't dare.
Wanted them starkers, artfully thrown,
like clay against the wall. More than

the Catholic girls wanted them, girls
who scrapped behind the cathedral over boys
other boys wanted. Wanted them despite
our mothers' warnings, those barefaced
liars who refused to admit they'd also
wanted boys who'd brought them

to the reservoir, and then to their knees.
Wanted them, not knowing
it would take the rest of our lives
to get over them – what they said to us,
what they did with their tongues. We were
obsessive, insufferable, chained ourselves

to them the way eco-warriors chain themselves
to bulldozers and trees. What choice
did we have but to trap them
the way we'd once trapped frogs,
ducklings, other forms of innocent
swamp life. They played us for suckers

and fools and still we went back,
wanting. Boys. Just boys.
God help us, we were doomed
before we began, hard-wired to want
even the loudmouth punks
setting off firecrackers at dawn.

Karita in Love (Again)

Gone three hours
but here she is, ambling up the driveway,
past the tool shed, swinging a goose

neck lamp. How dumb
my sister's face, heavy eyelids,
gold-dust blink, cupid-struck, a sloppy smile.

I don't have to ask.
I know something wildly
                              geometric
occurred at the lamp shop, something
grey and rectangular, streaked and smeared
blue and yellow. All that light!
There are days

when my sister wakes too early or late,
when she kneels on the ground, ripping up
buttercups with her teeth but not
today.
        Today
lilac stinks up the air
and I ask, So,

who is it this time, Karita?
Is it the lamp shop boy
with the soul-patch chin,
the operatic mouth?

Sophie's Lament

Nobody wants to be my boyfriend.
Nobody wants to walk through the cemetery to bring me dead tulips.
Who'll kiss my neck, bite my shoulder?
Who'll fall on his knees,
howl my name into the storm?
Life is not a fairytale! Though I *am* bewitching.
Dipped in darkness, I smell like the stars.
This cloistered life, these rooms full of books.
Stuff the peppers, light the candles, but where's the boy
who'll run his tongue down my spine,
the boy to sweeten this bitter stalk?

Harridans everywhere!
I see them in drawstring pants,
at grocery checkouts, hauling meat and toilet
paper from their carts. A man somewhere
loves each hausfrau's lizard skin.
Too soon I'll wither, a dry seed rattling inside
an old cigar box. If love is insanity, where's
the madman who'll swim my lunatic sea?
Does nobody want to be my boyfriend?
No teeth marks on my shoulder?
Not one dead tulip in the rain?

Questions to Ask Before Marriage: Tofino, BC.

Have you disclosed your mental-health histories,
the ghostly deer that haunted your ancestors,
men and women who still wander
among the dripping stalks of fennel?
Do you listen to each other's
complaints before they sink
below the surf? Children
or no children? If yes,
who will carry their tired bodies
across the bridge on wet summer nights?
Do your ideas about money and the mad chirping
in the underbrush
mesh? Will you expose your children
to nurse logs and bracket fungus? Who
will scoop up the fog that pours in from the ocean
like cream? When walking the beach,
do you stop and look into each other's eyes,
those sea stars buzzing life?
Do you love the way
his/her hiking boots turn dark with dew?
Will a television dominate the bedroom
or will you sleep on a mat of moss?
Do you value each other's friends,
the ones living in driftwood shacks, surfboards out front?
Are there things you're not prepared to give up –
arbutus trunks, quails thrashing through
salal outside your kitchen door?
When the time comes, will you step back,
allow your children to pass into the spruce forest?
To advance the other's career, would you
agree to move far from this place,
or would you sit neck-deep
in the river and suck on a stone?

Wedding Party

That was the morning the girl ditched
her textbooks behind the rosemary bush
before hitchhiking into town in ripped jeans

to meet her boyfriend in an elevator riding
up to the third floor of a stone building
where a Justice of the Peace raised his eye-

brows but went ahead anyhow, *till death
do us, in sickness and in health.* And that
was the night the newlyweds and their four

guests celebrated the occasion of their
elopement at the Kon-Tiki Restaurant on
Broughton Street, shut down a week later

after rats were seen scuttling across the foyer,
brazen as daylight, and a family of Texans
was poisoned en masse. The night the guests

ordered cocktails with names like *South Sea
Oblivion*, though the best woman, lacking
fake ID, was offered instead a virgin margarita,

and the best man, already famous for his
convoluted digressions, stood up to make
a rambling tribute to love but got sidetracked

by a thought of the potter's wheel in his
mother's basement. She'd threatened to send
all his stuff to the Sally Ann, so he needed

a truck, did anyone know anyone with a truck
he could borrow? And that was the night
a sense of doom fell over a wedding party

despite the double shots of rye and chunks
of strange meat floating in bowls, night the
bride and groom would look back on for

years, water trickling from a hole in the faux
rock wall, and everyone's future an exotic
island, unspoiled, and a long way off.

Sex Addict at the Surfside Motel

Don't tell me I don't want what I want
when I know that I want
to swing in the dumb arms of bliss.
With every new man I fly
in darker and darker circles.
A body is so many sad holes.
Should I try to explain what I want,
why I want, that I *am*
my libido, a long convulsive sob?
That I've driven three hours
into the desert at the end of a workday,
truck wheels shuddering?
It happens.
I meet them online,
big-talking no-shows who can't shake
their conscience or wives.
Stood up again.
Alone in a room with a bottle
of Scotch and bowl of stale peanuts, no,
not alone. In the parking lot
a big blond preacher's smoking a joint.
I lean on the sill, watch him squeeze
the roach between finger and thumb.
The minutes are long.
The ocean's a thousand miles away.
Heat pins small animals beneath it.
He looks up. Meets my eye.
The hair on the back of my neck
shimmies like feathery mesquite.

The adobe walls soften, twist
out of shape, and I want nothing
but that raw-boned God-man
speaking in tongues.

Sex: Reasons for Having It

I felt sorry for him, he was in a rut, we were celebrating someone's
birthday, shots of tequila, and – click – this profound
connection. She had brown eyes.
He had a way about him.
I wanted to experience God, sidle up to the Divine.
The night was long, she was a fox, I was a possum, the river was rough.
I thought it would improve my complexion.
It was my duty, wasn't it?
My mother said not to.
I was afraid he'd have an affair.
We were in Budapest.
When I walked into the room,
she was lying on her back, a field of black earth.
I fell into a trance.
I wanted to be plucked like a bug from the grimy windshield of life.
I was lonely.
He reminded me of a distant childhood triumph,
a race I couldn't stop running,
chain-link fence, blue ribbon, bloody nose.
I thought – I really *really* thought – it would boost my rep.
She was manic as the primary colours.
He asked nicely.
I wanted to stop the knock-knock jokes.
My investments had gone belly up.
She had this irresistible trailer-trash beauty.
It helped me sleep.
He winked.
It was the nineties.
I wanted to lock onto his extreme vibrations.
In her presence I sensed a sweet-stirring wind.
He was hopelessly tongue-tied
but whoa his body could speak these long digressive sentences

replete with extended, even pointless, metaphors that evoked
the sorrow I'd experienced only in dreams.
She was smart enough to be suspicious of me.
It was a cry for help.
You can cheat death by drowning three times,
then it's gimme the water wings.
He started to tell a malignant story that grew benign in its telling.
I wanted a raise, a favour, an excuse to quote Susan Sontag.
He was an enlightened exotic and I a degenerate Philistine.
Celibacy was as boring as the revenge of the intellect upon art.
You're okay, she said, which made it okay.
I wanted to feel trivial again, like a charm bracelet or banana split.
I thought it would promote hair growth.
He offered me a cigarette.
Her mind was a gorgeous bog of despair in which I longed to wallow.
You look like a nasty do-it-yourself project, he said.
Which aroused me. Which made me feel noble.
I wanted to wipe the smirk off my ex's face.
It hit me: soon I'd be worm food.
We arrived at the party in the same cowboy getup:
holsters, stirrups, chaps, lassos, the whole S&M bit.
I finally understood there's no relationship between what happens in bed
and what happens inside the head of the people in that bed.
It was a dare.
I was flattered.
She was so out of my league.
I read that it aerated the blood.
I wanted the walls to collapse, no east, no west, you know, like Berlin.
It was one of those days, a Tuesday, I think.
I was slumming.
It's cold in here, he said, we could make tea or we could make . . .
love? she said.

Interpretation

So much has been written about the dream
we don't know what it means anymore.
Though we do remember the dream had babies
and high heels and cocktails that levitated.
The men in the dream were talking
about cisterns, they didn't know what else
to talk about, while upstairs the women uncorked
bottles of fizzy pink wine. And then
we were inside a rundown summer house on a lake.
There was a lot of work to do,
sweeping and scrubbing, goddamn maggots.
We remembered the dream had a bar, cherry-topped drinks.
We kept sneaking little sips!
The floors so slippery the old dog slid on its belly
all the way to the burned-out wharf.
A rat turned into a Victorian poet in a buckskin jacket.
He was destitute, needed cash now.
Some said the dream meant creativity, others
that freedom was nigh. No one could agree.
It was a mess. It was pretty straightforward.
And then CJ showed up in a golf cart.
Beware of tiny hemlock trees, she said,
and other woody plants that take root in the lungs.

Why Helsinki

Because you were filled with the light of perpetual longing.
Because the open-air market,
pickled herring, birch branch bundles.
Because the whiz and whir of kitchen appliances
all over northern Europe.
Your brain sang like a bag of bees,
heart clanged like a bell tower.
What was going on?
Why this flea-bitten dog
trying to hump your human leg?
The kids in the square lurched and backfired,
their vodka-fuelled sputterings
more lyrical than anatomical.
Late June, rutting season, a mongrel dog hot on your tail.
Because a white cathedral, neoclassical columns, five green domes,
the dog trailing you past Kauppatori Square,
around the boy sitting upright on a bench,
drunk and asleep in blinding sunlight.
Because you climbed the church steps, then turned
and kicked the dog hard before ducking inside.
Ten minutes, twenty, half an hour.
Because each time you peeked through a crack in the door,
there it was – four-legged mutt hunkered down,
chin on front paws.
Because your deep animal shame.
The dog patient as any good lover.

A Brief History of Rape

Before we knew loneliness
you were the loneliest
thing to lurch across the horizon.
Or was it a trick of the light?
Were you really some other animal,
stunned by the song of horns butting horns?

*

The moment you could walk
upright, you set to
hauling rock, dragging trees,
pounding metal. You couldn't help
yourself, all those holes
you had to dig in the earth, sticks
of dynamite shoved into its crevices.
Where we saw filth and destruction, you saw
a trajectory, clean as a tornado.

*

You threw up buildings,
turned on the air conditioning.

In a smoky bar we brushed against you.
Do you come here often?

You did.
You came for no good reason.

*

Anatomical opposite, muscular twin
sentient other, a-
moral equivalent, all
that we were only more
deadly.

*

Of course we grew moody.
Of course pearls for their own sake.
Every night warming to your hands,
opening our legs. The weight of you
rising and falling like a drill rig.

*

Monster, nitwit, trollop.
You tossed back names
and still we followed you
down winding staircases, into
libraries and art galleries.
Hair piled high, hips swaying.

*

Dismiss you, ignore you, explain you away?
Impossible! Every time we tried
we were dumbstruck: the curve
of your spine, your jawbone's
accidental beauty.

*

By anatomical opposite I mean
man, fixed gender, dogma, religion
thou shalt and *shalt not.* I mean a bat
flying out of your ear, chittering like a prophet.

*

When we woke
the worst thing was in motion.
Go, we said. *Go away.*
But you kept sliding toward us
over ladders and balcony railings.
The worst thing
about to happen.
Did happen.
Happens.
Does.

Scene of Blame

The man.
The woman watching the man.
The man in the barn's shadow watching the girl
on the fence every day after school.

The horse galloping across the field.
The window through which the woman looks.
Day's last light.
The seeing and the seen.
The horse the girl cares for
but does not care
to ride.

On this she is adamant.
On this she won't negotiate.

Despite the man's disappointment.
Despite the woman's move from the city.

The girl's brush strokes and rubdowns.
Oats and sweet hay. The raised hind leg.
The stones picked out of the hooves.
The curry comb, the mane and tail.

The man turning toward the house.
The woman on the other side of the glass.
The sacrifices and considerable expense.

The girl. The paddock. The stable.
The unused saddle, riding boots, stirrups, etc.

The unridden horse, its cantering body.

Man in the Moon Arrives on the Red-Eye

Striding across the tarmac,
you were already talking eclipse, talking lunacy,
whistling *Werewolves of London.*

On the drive into town
your appearance kept changing,
one minute a pumpkin, the next a trombone.
Like all drinking men,
you wept egg-shaped tears.
And your smile, autumnal and helpless,
as you sat at the kitchen table,
recalling Springfield, Missouri, 1939,
the night you fell from the sky.

You were so jetlagged you let me feed you
as though you were a child,
cheese slices, a plastic cup of juice.
Cheap drugstore glasses
balanced on the ridge of your nose.
Your cheeks were shadow-pocked craters,
your eyes seas of frozen lava.

All month I left notes on your crescent-shaped pillow:
When you leave me,
will you fly into the gorgeous scree of heaven?
Will you lose yourself the way rain
loses itself in an emerald pool?

Still, we planned for the future –
Stonehenge, the caves of Lascaux.
Played cat and mouse, marked the dark side of sex
on an ancient lunar calendar. But I knew it would end,

it was all a celestial illusion, the honeymoon
and elk-calling, the giant toads
swallowing themselves whole.

The evening of your departure the tides maxed out
and you seemed to be waning.
On the doorstep,
you kissed me goodbye and then,
for no reason, balanced on one leg, arms wide,
a fish in your beak.

Your sudden whimsy brighter than
all the poems written in eighth-century China.
Or the moon-soaked words of the wine-quaffing Li Po.

The Long Marriage

She studies his forehead, its frontal eminence, curve
that slides into a dome where his hair recedes.
The ridge above his eyes: superciliary arch.
Glabella: the space between them.

A candle, thin-crust pizza, bottle of red wine.
From where she's sitting in the restaurant with burnt
orange walls his right temporal crest is thrown
into shadow. She shakes salt onto the table.
Granules bounce and scatter.
Salt, he says, *you eat too much salt.*

The horizontal folds on his forehead bunch over
arches that flow down around his temples.
The outside of his left eye socket:
orbital margin of the zygomatic bone.

When did he develop crow's feet?
When did she?

On either side of his face, a chewing muscle.
She follows the maxilla back to the highest point of his ear.
They continue to eat in silence.
Outside, snow tornadoes spin
on the sidewalk: winter sprites.
The end of another meal in a lifetime of meals together.
She pushes her plate aside, leans forward on her elbows,
regards his jawbone's contour as he
signals for the bill.

Nose: asymmetrical, broken as a child.
Alae: nostrils' wings. Mouth: the crease where lips fuse
downward. His father's lips: labial commissures.
Philtrum: little channel connecting nose
to the centre of cupid's bow.

He drains the wine bottle: *Ready to go?*
Lids like skin on custard float over eyeballs on the face
she's observed up close for four decades,
face grown old without her noticing, become
sculpture, face so familiar she thinks
upon waking it's her own face: assemblage
of muscle, cartilage, connective tissues.
His skull, her bones.

On the Night of the Apocalypse
Yahweh Tickles the Ivories

The fifth child was male so our mother named him Yahweh,
for he had no beginning and no end. Stars fell on Alabama,

but in her thousand eyes he moved like jazz in a swing coat,
a swing coat dressed up in leaves that rustled *mercy, mercy*.

She turned her head this way and that, trying to take him in,
her birdland boy, her lucky so-and-so, trying to see the one who

moved too fast to be seen. While she went ja-da for our brother,
we strapped on roller skates, roared up and down the chalky

streets in porkpie hats. Worry about our mother, why worry?
Hadn't Yahweh stayed to feed her fags and cold black tea?

Years passed in a guilty, sentimental mood. We misbehaved, we
got around. We forgot our mother's stardust tears, forgot that once

she'd loved her satin dolls, her Ipanema girls, forgot until the night
Yahweh called us home to Dolphin Street. *Those ill winds?* he crooned,

don't mean a thing, and we, such fools (North, South, East, West),
her pale and feckless daughters, gathered like a summer storm.

Grief

I wore it for more than a year like a second skin
unaware of what it was

(flannel nightgown, red cardigan, puce T-shirt)
the piece of clothing I washed by hand

unaware of what it was
I'd drape it over the radiator

the piece of clothing I washed by hand
that shapeless rag

I draped over the radiator
the night I observed myself in the cheval mirror

this shapeless rag, I said to myself
I must have taken it from my mother's closet after she died

in the cheval mirror I observed myself
in the flannel nightgown (red cardigan, puce T-shirt?)

I took from my mother's closet after she died
and wore for more than a year like a second skin.

Over Lunch I Ask Three Friends
What Their Mothers Said to Them About Sex

It was a funny way for God to arrange things.

Would you like to see my diaphragm?

Here's the book on chickens.

Sign of the Times

The last elephant on earth took apart the house
we'd spent our lives building. Board by board and nail by nail.
She sang as she ducked electrical cables and phone lines,
a harrowing song to a scorched earth. The tip of her trunk
so delicate not a window was broken, not a plate
or wineglass. At last we could see into the rooms
we'd lived in for years, empty but for an abandoned
wasps' nest. Mardi Gras celebrants paraded past
and so did the family living next to the nuclear power plant.
Baby and dog glowed like those fluorescent green frogs
that sprang from the earth that wet, wet autumn.
And there were our children, running through Barker's Field,
climbing the oak trees, stealing eggs from their nests –
sparrowhawks, buzzards, red kites, corn buntings.
We wanted to believe in their innocence but in the cold
brightness of the moment knew they were thieves.
All this happened years ago, and still we wake in a house
without ceilings or walls, windows or wineglasses, the flutter
of ghost-wings in the rafters, a deep infrasonic warbling.

Death

I woke and saw a scarecrow in a field of eucalyptus
and the oil from the leaves bled into the light
and the light was blue. The scarecrow reached,
palms to the sky, as though waiting for something –
the gooseberries to ripen, the sun to turn to ash? –
waited in his bandana and wisdom until seven
rosellas alighted on his head and shoulders.
And I too was a raggedy creature made of chicken
wire and knotted string and each time a gang-gang
cockatoo pecked at my skull, I flinched and cried
and swivelled in the empty blue space cobbled together
out of buttons and kite tails. I squatted on the ground
and listened to the scarecrow talk until I was transfigured
by his words the way I'd once been transfigured by
your words, made stronger, more whole. The straw man
grew bright in his pigments as I leaned against him that cool
October evening, my joints stiff with tapioca paste. And
O beloved, every time I thought of you in that attic room,
an old man holding on to his brokenness, the crows threw
up a great caterwauling that flayed the air like butcher cord,
and the butcher cord beat the mute air senseless.

Endgame

Evolutionarily, [Elizabeth Gould] Davis argued that parthenogenesis was not only our origin as a species but our ultimate destiny. —SALON

The earth hiccupped, contracted
spasmodically and it was
all over. We tried to warn you,
even put up signs – *Don't show your face
round here no more* – but you

underestimated our ruthlessness,
couldn't believe we'd hit on
a winning formula –
immaculate conception, fast-lane
procreation. We became

explosive,
independently fertile,
invasive,
a new species.

Your shocked expression
as we herded you into tar sands and deserts,
pushed you into oceans, those open sewers.
Cut you off at the knees, drowned
you in your own bathwater.
We wrote you out

of our script and ecosystem,
cancelled you from the equation
and called it a vanishing act, evolution,
metamorphosis, called you on the phone

but you were futzing with your riflescopes
and rangefinders, your hi-tech infrared optics.

What choice did we have?
You were a future
we could not inhabit.
Nature's endgame,
Y-chromosomed,
defective loverboy.

*

Time has snuffed out constellations
and still we turn restless circles each spring.
We raise our voices and young in the amorphous colonies.
We go forth, multiplying in our own image,
mourning what we do not know, your footsteps
among the citrus groves, mourning the sweetheart
in you, the darling boy with his curious gaze
and litany of questions, boy in his superman costume,
uptilted face as his mother presses
the damp curl to his forehead.

*

The rooms swarm with soil-hued animals.
By candlelight we drink raw turnip beer.
The rafters squawk with birds and twilight
has fingers that never stop moving.
If this makes no sense to you,
look, the child in the doorway,

wavy chevron markings
on either side of her head,
turquoise tail, little gold skirt
spun from unspun vegetable fibre.

*

Every myth bleeds into a memory of you.
Our bruises are vestigial, and our dreams –
riderless horses – stand very still.

Torso

Every now and then another prehistoric
sweetheart bubbles up through
the sediment in one sexually
explicit piece, smelling
of mud and honeysuckle.
This time it's me, pocket-
sized Venus caked in geology, first
in a long line carved out of mammoth tusks.
So what if my arms are tiny
daggers, my legs diminutive stumps?
So what if my head's absurdly
disproportionate, smaller than a pea?
Wash the clay from my belly,
brush my thighs clean.
A toothpick will pluck the grit
from between my breasts.
My vulva's so contemporary
it's almost pornographic.
Distinguished paleoanthropologists,
night arrives, as it does, moist and fragrant,
and I remember the eons of silence,
earthworms sliding between my thighs.
I thought about nothing in the bell-shaped
dark, nothing but dirt. In the end,
how it covers everything.

God's Last Words

On Sex and Wooden Boats: God's Last Words

1.

Open your mouth. And I said it again: Open.
For nothing's as strange as the mouth giving or

receiving a kiss. And let your restraint be record-
setting. Let your passion smoulder for seven days

and seven nights on a double-ender with a smooth
cutaway forward and deep keel aft. Yea, for the

terrible longing that afflicts the lowly also afflicts
the mighty. Therefore, let each one offer consolation

unto the other. To this end, fasten your framework
of ribs to a keelson shaped from sturdy fir timbers.

2.

And fear not, for I shall not smite you for bedding
down one with the other or for entering into communion

with the one whom you adore. Behold, for I, even I,
am the breath of the wind that carries your dory up

the Inside Passage and through the misty fjords.
Moreover, I myself built by hand a fifty-foot vessel

out of overlapping planks that I might traverse the inlets
and narrow channels and also bless the open sea. And

do not lust after the beauty of angels, for they are not
of your kind. Nor should you rush after saviours with

3.

bony appendages, for they are false prophets
who would sojourn two score and six years on

your fibreglass catamaran, smoking your cigarettes
and drinking your wine. No, it would be better that

you build for your sons and your daughters a modest
rig with a low cabin and two solar panels. Ask yourselves:

is it right that a man or woman remains alone at the
helm day after day, controlling the umber-coloured

sails? Rather, let each one tarry in the beloved's
berth, then rise up like the stern's upward swing.

4.

For whoever stands in shallow water, stands on
holy ground, for I am God, creator of every seaworthy

craft, yea, even those built out of red-cedar planks on
yellow-cedar frames. And it came to pass that a man

and woman sailed toward the harbour in a little skiff,
and the skiff was named *Arbutus Girl*, and it was

adorned with sachets of balm and spices and myrrh,
and lo, the man and woman's laundry hung on the mast

like strips of bark beaten flat against stone. And the man
offered unto me an oarlock and pulley made from hard

5.

wood, but I protested, saying, Keep for yourself every
quart of tung oil to preserve the fir stave that supports

the mainsail, and in high seas remember always to weigh
down your ballast. But if the hull is shallow and the rudder

balanced, know therefore that the skiff shall abide from
one generation unto the next. And I saw that the man

had laboured all his days, building *Arbutus Girl*, so I said
unto him, As the sun rises and sets, so shall you sail

according to the seasons, whereupon I pricked my thumb
with a sewing awl, and my blood rained upon the seas,

6.

staining the water the colour of rust. And I spoke no
more unto the man, yea, not a word did I speak,

for my eyes had turned toward the woman as
she navigated within inches of the rocky shore,

and between the closely anchored boats. And I saw
that the desire of one for the other continued,

until all flesh was driven to distraction. And so I said,
Let the woman teach the man to steer by the stars,

and let the man teach the woman to fashion a dinghy
out of half-inch plywood. And I was perplexed by

7.

their lovemaking, that it was more vigorous during
the hurricane season than during the long calm crossings.

And so I said, Let there be moon but not lamentation.
Let each one cup the face of the other in both palms.

But lo, what is that sound tunnelling down through
the strait – flapping sails? water cicadas? weeping?

And I said, Lift up your eyes and look upon the petroglyphs
incised on the cliff's surface for their joy is naked and

splendid and the sea is full and the salmon return
always from whence they came. And I said, Is there

8.

any sort of sex about which it can be said, See,
this is new? I asked this question but no answer

was given, for the people understood: everything
that is, is already old. And so I said, Let there be

double-jointed sex and sex using both halves of
the brain. Let it occur with or without eye contact,

while envisioning shiny rotating objects. Let there
be exuberance in the spacious galleys and five-ton

cargo holds. Moreover, do not harass one another,
for this one or that one must come unto you willingly

9.

and with honest desire. And I said, Let there be
floating lanterns and also kayaks named after birds:

osprey and Arctic tern. Therefore, cast your love upon
the water and do not cry out in hunger, for within three

days your love shall return to you ninefold in the body
of a pink fish. And feast together, taking only your portion,

and afterwards, undress and lie down and say, Truly
the light through the porthole is the colour of watermelon.

Say: My love is a pleasure to know in watermelon light.
Who among you remembers the antediluvian times

10.

when all things were formless and fury roamed about
my face and my anger was a constant drumbeat against

the firmament? In those days I was unsure of my plans,
so built models to test the design of every shape and

manner of human. And my replicas, yea, my upright
miniatures, even *they* longed for union and completeness.

And so I said, Let seven battened sails separate light
from darkness, for the humans are irrepressible and

more ravenous than even I could have imagined.
And I communed with my own heart until I knew

11.

beyond a doubt that I was God, originator of all things,
yea, even the square sail for running the trade winds,

even the junk's scooping deckline. And I bent toward
earth on a quiet afternoon to watch the men and women

construct their handcrafted sloops beneath orange
tarps, and they sensed my presence and thus did they

ask me: Why do the winds blow toward the south and
turn toward the north and whirl about without ceasing?

And I answered: Because the yew tree dreams paddles.
Because the yuloh births prayers. And I continued:

12.

If desire distracts you in your middle years, consider
the dog barking on the dock and the children in the culverts,

consider even them, before plunging headlong into the deep.
And I said, Why do you appear before the beloved clothed

in selfishness? Rather, you must give unto this or that
one as the clouds give rain that they might bring forth

the blueberries where the sand meets the forest's edge.
And I said to the women, Let there be shoes for your feet

and a comely stranger walking in your midst. And lo,
there he goes now with pulleys and cable, manoeuvring

13.

a thirty-foot cutter through the trees and down a steep
slope onto the muddy beach. And let the taste of first sex

be as sweet as the hull's first taste of water. Whosoever
remembers the beginning, remembers that once I

ordered Noah to build an ark out of gopher wood, but
now I've grown soft as goat's cheese. Now I say, Bring

unto me the men who love men and the women who
love women, that I might say: Choose freely and with

a full heart whomsoever you choose. And I said, Let
there be choice. Let the choices multiply and fill the earth.

14.

Let sex occur in humble vessels with or without oars,
and let the oars carved with simple tools (saw, axe, chisel)

feather the coastal waters. And I saw how inventive your
lovemaking had become, so I said, Let every gaff-rigged

ketch sail to and from the green islands, yea, let
diversity reign. And it came to pass that your brains

could calibrate more angles than a sextant, and so I
looked down upon a summer morning and said unto

you: I know not how or why but I like you best when
you go out upon the waters in your little wooden boats.

Acknowledgements

The first section of the book owes a debt to Havelock Ellis and his six-volume, thirty-one-year project, *Studies in the Psychology of Sex* (1887–1928), from which I have lifted quotations that intrigued, amused, amazed, outraged, moved or somehow inspired me to write a poem. Images or phrases drawn from Ellis's work are occasionally woven into the poems themselves. More often, however, a quotation simply triggered the writing of the poem that follows. In some cases, the process was reversed: I wrote a poem, and then sought out a quotation that I felt illuminated, enlarged or gave context to the words.

I wrote "The Problem of Describing Scent" after reading Robert Hass's "The Problem of Describing Color."

I would like to thank the Canada Council for the Arts, the British Columbia Arts Council and the University of New Brunswick for their support during the writing of this manuscript. Thanks also to the following magazines in which some of these poems first appeared: *Arc, CV 2, Event, The Fiddlehead, Geist, Grain, The Malahat Review, Liminus, The New Quarterly, Poetry Ireland Review, Prairie Fire, Prism International* and *Room of One's Own.*

A selection of poems from the first section of the book, "The Art of Love," was shortlisted in the CBC literary competition in 2010.

"What We Know about Babies" placed second in *Prairie Fire*'s Bliss Carmen poetry competition, and was reprinted in *Geist.*

"Night-Running," published in *CV 2,* has been chosen for inclusion in *The Best Canadian Poetry in English* (Tightrope Books, 2010), edited by Lorna Crozier.

"The Tulip Tree" placed second in *Room of One's Own*'s poetry contest, and "An Auto-Erotic History of Swings" received an honourable mention.

"Dildo" and "Brass Eggs" were shortlisted in *Arc*'s Poem of the Year Contest.

"Boys" was published in *Rocksalt: An Anthology of Contemporary B.C. Poetry* (Mother Tongue Publishing, 2008), edited by Mona Fertig and Harold Rhenisch.

"Sex: Reasons for Having It" won *Grain*'s prose poem competition.

"The Long Marriage" was shortlisted for *The Malahat Review*'s Open Season Award.

"On the Night of the Apocalypse Yahweh Tickles the Ivories" won *Arc*'s Poem of the Year Contest.

"Grief" was published in *Have a Heart,* a chapbook edited by Amy Ainbinder.

"Sign of the Times" received an honourable mention in *The Fiddlehead*'s poetry contest.

"On Sex and Wooden Boats: God's Last Words" was shortlisted for the *Malahat Review*'s Long Poem Contest and published in *Prairie Fire*.

I would like to thank the wonderful women in my writing groups, lfc and the fb – Lucy Bashford, Lisa Baldiserra, Laurel Bernard, Dede Crane, Jennifer Fraser, Claudia Haagen, Penny Hocking, Barbara Henderson, Eve Joseph, Cynthia Kerkham, Carol Matthews, Jill Margo, Janice McCachen, Arleen Paré and Julie Paul – for their camaraderie and the nights of food and wine and poetry.

Thanks also to my long-time friend and editor, Michael Kenyon, for his keen eye and big heart.

And finally, thanks to my husband, Terence, first and foremost and always.

PATRICIA YOUNG has published nine collections of poetry and one of short fiction. She has won numerous awards for her poetry, including the Pat Lowther Memorial Award, the Dorothy Livesay Award, the Bliss Carmen Award, the National Magazine Award, the League of Canadian Poets' National Poetry competition and *Arc*'s Poem of the Year Contest. Two of her collections have been shortlisted for the Governor General's Award for Poetry. *Airstream*, her collection of short fiction, received the inaugural Rooke-Metcalf Award and was shortlisted for the Butler Prize and named one of *The Globe and Mail*'s best books of the year. In 2009 and 2010, selections of her poetry were shortlisted for the CBC literary competition.

Patricia Young has two grown children and lives in Victoria, B.C. with her husband, the writer Terence Young.